Happy You Are Here

Happy You Are Here

POEMS

Ayaz Pirani

THE WORD WORKS
WASHINGTON, D.C.

Address inquiries to:
THE WORD WORKS
P.O. Box 42164
Washington, D.C. 20015
editor@wordworksbooks.org

Cover: Susan Pearce Design
Author photograph: Afreen Malik

LCCN: 2015960103
ISBN: 978 -1-944585-06-8

Acknowledgments

These poems first appeared in the following journals:

ARC: "Love Song"
Cranky Literary Journal: "Tipping Points"
Josephine Quarterly: "Next-Life Anxiety Complex"
Poetry Midwest: "Bedtime"
White Leaf Review: "Poem by Mario Praz (1896 - 1982)"
     (titled "Advice to a Student")

Thank you, Barbara Orlovsky, Kyle Vaughn, and Nancy White.

Contents

I.

II.

III.

IV.

for Afreen

His temperament the nightingale's
His task the salamander's

—Ghalib

I've been thinking
of you in my country.
I bet you lie down just fine.
I know you want to
see the conscious forest.
We'll do that tomorrow.
Also the lions in trees.
For now go ahead
and take me in your arms.
This place's God
is loving.

I.

Friendship

Gentle fable this,
stubborn with secrets and
mysteries of Nature.

When He gives the signal about
our own lives we'll never know.

They say if you put your
heart into describing
a rose the space you occupy
gets bigger and more
people get blown away
in your love's Sphere.

You end up putting a stamp
on the Earth.

Being in This World

Synonyms for flesh are
fine-edged, like bee-wing.

How like the leaf's curl it is
being in this world
of diminishing returns.

Memory and mimicry,
secret tasks formed from
a lost this and that.

If I change the image
will the tyrant return?

It isn't possible,
this destroying,
unless it is your plan

to make of me what
can be made of me.

I thought you'd already
know the things I have lost.

It's your turn to whip me.

Immigrant Astronaut

I can't get over being on Earth.

It helps that I'm with you but who knows
what you see in me
                              or place in me
each time I'm near your fragrance?

I'm getting up from this chair.
I haven't stood up from it before
but I'm standing now
and by that I mean no harm.

It's just that you've put in the hard work.
Go ahead and say the words

that you'll never hear me say
which explains my face.

My mouth is a hummingbird's lodge.
He took up residence in me
when I came to the New World. That's

when all my color flew inward
                              and I grew neutral and flagless

iridescent only on the inside.

Pub Speech, Queensbury Arms, Toronto, 1988

One remembers to lock the self's door.
Who sets out to talk about
himself without disguise?
I wanted to pay my tribute
to the lakes of Ontario,
having matured in the surrounding
straw-colored tussocks[1]—
my brown eyes full of heart
and little black pate
cotton-soft like shoddy.[2]
We have more or less of that
snow of which I spoke
and which always astonishes
the oaks and the hazel spinneys.[3]
A great deal of life
is conquering Faith to know
for what purpose is this mischief?
I can say I've loved putting
my beak in the water.
Apt to take big bites.
Apt as a child to destroy[4]
what it admires:
He who knows instantly—
that old Greek belief.

---

1   Robert Palfrey Utter, "Winter Mist"
2   Harry Esty Dounce, "Some Nonsense About a Dog"
3   Hilaire Belloc, "The Mowing of a Field"
4   Rupert Brooke, "Niagara Falls"

I'm Going into the Burning Building

That's what you do when
your love is dead—
you go looking for lashes.

You find out how
many degrees Jupiter
is from the moon.

This is how
you make the knots
she wrote in her ginan.
I'm not one of those
things that lies down
wherever it is put, she added.

Now you know why
I will never come back.
I know my rights—

requisite that I let go of
my life's work,
find the first place
touched by her ways.

II.

Tipping Points

Snow, plowed to my door: thaw!
I told you my mouth is a hummingbird's lodge.
That last one's beauty. If only
I could make it to the Ngorongoro Crater
and empty my pockets.
No living woman can compete
with Rita Hayworth. Curry my boiled lentils.
Strike this match anywhere.
Essay topic: *origin of the kiss*.
It was her dark hair. The red oak
from the kitchen window.
Gunshot in Sarajevo. Mosque in Samarra.

Bettyes Guest House, Santo Domingo

Inky fingerprinted bedfellows.
Our lip-biting abandoned
with news of the day—
drone strikes limbless girl.

A speck I say which
is less than a scent you say.
No more than a fourth
of a glance. Blotted, stamped.
Not even half a chance.

Into the bluegreen patch of
gross exposure we fling and swim.

Poem by A.M. Sullivan (1830 -1884)

Nay but when the earth shall be crushed with crushing on crushing

—SURA LXXXIX

I burst at last to pieces!

You see, He had maps of
the Transvaal and of Cyprus
and the harbors of Famagousta,
Limasol, and all the rest of it.

Then came the *seat of war*
in Afghanistan, which covered
all that remained of the wall.

Freed from fears are they
who see Him face to face—

a Taskmaster's eye
dodging crooked, then
transfigured, dodging back.

Father, bomber, country.

Girl Without Limbs

Not impurities alone are burnt in the fire.
Buds and blossoms too are blackened.
                        —Ambai

There was another girl—
a beggar. She did
have her legs
but no arms.
I wondered how they
had come off?
Seven myself at
Good Morning Paan
she lay on cardboard
like a doll dropped from
a dog's mouth.

Things of Peace

She is ill, lying on the orange sofa
when I visit the home. I punch up the
dead flowers in my useless bouquet—
the petals flying to sources underground.

Look! You were a dark-haired beauty
in this photograph, taken by Lake Manyara.
Next slide: of lions, indolently arboreal;
things of peace, confounding signature.

For them her mouth opens—a providence.
Drink this water, take this tablet.
Ignore the pink rush of petals to the floor.
Down-eider, hairs of God.

Gift Shop

In La Romana tourist kids
frothed around the beach
amputating starfish. We smiled
at them to see if
they recognized two special people.
Honeymooners.
Avengers against the negative spin
Earth had taken.

But when the kids looked at us
brown and woodenly posed
in our bathing suits,
we felt indigenous
of inexplicit kind, like
factory-mades
for an eliminated people.

~[snow]~

time to eat nuts and bolts

from now until April
all the movies are in black and white
the novels on pages Bible-thin

they found a *Maid in the Marsh*

someone's daughter too I know

they fade in your heart
the throbs in your heart

(white) city   kid (tropic)

Space for Grief

At least I had the tasbih
as a kid in mosque.

Thirty-three beads of a tribe
strung in black thread
with a knot called a fumko
gathering potently in my hands.

Augural that we kissed
the fumko where
everything bottlenecks.

Explain 'Dead'

First she undressed
to her petticoat,
then she undressed me—
button, zipper, *leg up*.

Cold thigh-hairs,
then car horn and bark.
Crook of neck.

Uncle is dead
so I said *Explain 'dead'*
as she unbuttoned my chest,
made me sleeveless.

Love Song

Simple acts become ritual—
I first noticed this in my mother.
Because I woke early, maybe five
or six, walked in circles
on the landing, I could hear her
lay aside her blanket and my
father's hand in one long sweep
of her black hair. Now
I grieve for everything.
I looked at my father, asleep
on the other side of the bed,
in half-familiar light. I think
love is measured by degrees of light.
I sat on the dresser as my mother
brushed her hair. I think love
is measured by brushstrokes.
Later, in our yellow kitchen,
my mother and I had our own
separate journeys. At the table
I read big picture books while she
cut chicken in a silver bowl
by the sink. Tomato curry brewed
alongside the Earth-smell of
all-wheat chapattis. In
the afternoon I spread butter
over bread and over this I stroked
red currant jam. I laid the newspaper
open like scripture, for my father.
A simple act. I have written
all of my love songs in advance.

Old Friend

for Derick

Tangent and knotted as wreckage,
perilously brave, a wryness *ex libris*—
all bony, his manner is caesural.
Rhodesia, Tanganyika—for us, genital
as the deep, the forest, a fruit's fullness.
Colonialists, though—to our advantage?

Poem by Joseph Joubert (1754 -1824)

I never
like evergreen trees.
    Something black
    in their green, cold
    in their shade.
    Dry pointed prickly. Besides,
    they lose nothing
    and with nothing to fear
    seem without feeling.

Hundred Ways

My twin desires—
at mosque I grow devout
and tryst with
a calligraphist.
Our station under an
etched bismillah
deflects my best intentions.
She glorifies
Gabriel's scriptural river
while I count the
hundred ways
I could approach her neck.

Beak in the Water

The least to know
is what speck of
meaning is in our lives.

What dust our
needles catch?

You hope at
yawning Ngorongoro
to pick up Earth's beat

its paws of course being so mighty.

Ghalib

Ghalib asks
what do you know of
all that Ghalib endured?

His also was dark-
haired with silver
where God touched.

Each night is the last
when Ayaz loves completely
what frightens him.

Title-Poem

Moments when our starlit
spirit humanizes us.
Hair-tress or hand-sleight
all append to a narrative:
My Pinned Butterflies
and flipping through they constellate
into memory, fashioned.
Jackfruit. Boyhood.
Pleasure to meet you.

III.

Thank You

I used to write of the moon.

You couldn't tell if
it was waxing or waning
was the punch line. Of course

there was a sliver of truth
to the moon saving me.
It lit Montreal as I walked
crazily after a dose of medicine.

How or what you are
I don't know except
when full you are like
a cake Earthlings eat from.

Kabir

Kabir asks
at whom is Kabir shouting?

Some of you will just
pass by this poem
even though the woman
in it is a dark-haired beauty.

A poem that is one of
an infinite precipitation
she has caused.

In the spider's web
thoughts are pungent
Ayaz tells you.

Designer Baby

Hair-curls like quince petals,
pollinated cheeks.
Birthmark below left eye—
an X of beauty
proves even the most beautiful
are not gods.
Notice something about your fingers?
They hold on.
Everyone checks the box
for long eyelashes and takes big bites.
I liked heartbroken,
not heartbreaker.

Poem by Carl Van Doren (1885 -1950)

As an owl blinking in the dingy garret

discover with me what
a poise Hawthorne stood at:

the center of traveling entertainers,
minstrels and jongleurs,
the seldom-smiling.

Seize upon matters of Art
more than scrupulous tableaux.

There is a tough rustic fiber,
a hickory-hearted
yoke of dreams.

In his stony Province
things end with dry knowing.

All this and a crackling dialect
is yours from your perch
this evening.

Bedtime

When I speak without
gestures I feel empty, blank as
the beach in Marina.

Your father is quiet and gentle
as grape flesh.

Did you just spit out
the betel nut?

It is time for you
to love me. *Look, after all,*
as with any gesture.

Tucked away, my sweet fugitive,
lately?

Holiday in Necropolis

Now that we are back
from Egypt it won't help to look
at the big picture.

We'll ask each other, we'll ask ourselves.
The answer won't satisfy.

Knowing will not help
said His beard
about those that gave themselves
marigolds of trouble.

Oh my figment,
my playdate, tent-friend,
together on this, agreed?

Poem by Mario Praz (1896-1982)

Bandit-heroes are difficult to calculate.
I say weep and wring your hands.
Surrender to blankness.
Our species is not royal. On this
teenaged Byron's heart beat.
You can be of God's party
without knowing it.
Wear a kirpan, threaten your wrists.
Horse-laugh in Romantic agony.
With frost-bitten fingers rip
yourself a diorama of unhappiness.
Bejewel this boy and that.
Create nano-remembrances
with arm-hair love-knots.
Foxgloves, cloisters, too.
So many virgins!

Droid's Last Words

In this rose-wilting century the edges
of art burned as we approached.
Gone are the dark-haired beauties—
we are all cognates of a steel pinhead.
Our voices came to resemble cat purrs.
Inevitable then an automaton's jeremiad
for the last battery-charge of his species.

Act of Human Kindness

Aga Aly Shah hunted near Poona
with his old Persian corps
that fought in the Bolan.
The forest hem was deafened
by their dark exploits.
Those whose land he had taken
asked him why he hunted
deer they believed had souls.
He replied that the infirm
spoke to him, saying
they longed for easy death.

In the World War Between All Life on Earth

For when there shall be a trump on the trumpet...
                    —SURA LXXIV

We find the first leader credible
because of his bloodline. Perhaps
a small charming Navy youth from
which all his metaphors grow.
At a meeting like this he is epauletted.
Curls in his hair are man-made.
The second leader knows
tactical poisoning, throat cutting.
We owe him for pulling an armless girl
who was lost in a forest out of a fire.
Her pants were off, her lip broke.
He prefers eggplant colors.

Inside the room with the two big bellies
a table of fats and salts, lobster claws.
From the apple in the glazed pig
head's mouth a tree branch is knotted
with not-blossoms. Open window lets in
birds to its perches. That was how
easily the bombers slipped in
after Nature switched sides
having purchase everywhere of course.

Yaw Theory

Course undecided but hopeful
like a spill or a two-seater reaching
for the thermal, that little quiver of yaw
—a squeaky bum wiggle—
until the pilot commits the plane to his hand.

Sometimes there's a bit of a shiver
in us too, and we're not sure if
we'd rather be back on Earth.

A hummingbird that visits your garden
will fly right to your head
and hover if you stand still,
stare at you without comment.
This even our friends can't do.

Happy You Are Here

Hold to the light the stained glass
we found walking Max
in the oak woods of Arroyo Seco.
You too want to learn the fragment's provenance.
This nosiness makes me glad for both of us,
for all things on Earth
that get their noses into the piles
of Mystery the Maker's created.
I'm so happy you are here.

IV.

Written with the Other Hand

I don't need to
love a good whipping
to be a prophet
among my people.

I'm not choosing my words.

My people don't
want to know all
the things I've lost.

They had to go.

If my words are
penetrating
they're on their own.

Pub Speech, Wolverton Gardens, London, 1908

Last chance to remember.
How very few leaves will I really turn over,[5]
living in your cold, white world?
I go about my business in the rain.
Yesterday I received a telegram
delivered by a man in a monkey suit
instead of by a monkey.
This city doesn't have such miracles.
What's the point of gnashing teeth
and clawing air if
there's no forest to run into?
Luckily I did have a hat for my hands
to hold, a brim for rubbing.
The telegram is from my wife.
Look how it glows inside its envelope
like the tin of afterbirth
she and I buried under the kitchen in Kapsabet.
I don't need to read it.
Either like Anacreon with
grape in's throat
or like Hercules
with fire in's marrow,[6]
I've got to cross the ocean again.
Our girl is dead, the house is on fire,
the mangos fell before ripening.
Peas just won't get out of pod.
There's no point in staying.

---

5   William Penn, *The Fruits of Solitude*
6   Sir Thomas Overbury, "A Roaring Boy"

All I do is walk in and out of buildings.
My professors keep telling me
how long a way it is
from a cromlech to York Minster.[7]
No one is more alone on Earth
than the people in this city.

---

7   Ralph Waldo Emerson, *English Traits*

Saith the Lord

You're taking *multiply* too seriously.
I know children are like graven images
which are otherwise frowned upon.

You're taking *frowned upon* too seriously.
You think in the end I Who Turn Away
am really going to turn you away?

My Heart is made of your imagination.
You'll be blown away by its high fidelity.

Next-Life Anxiety Complex

If needed could I
call up a gale to
fling coconuts and
warn the villagers?
Could I descend the well
and bring back a corpse?
Keep the fires burning
in the streets on new moon?
Could I arrange for
a mottled horse, necessary
to marry the milkmaids
for the next fifty years?
Well, could I?
It doesn't seem likely.
My fingers are long but
belong in gloves,
good just for caresses.
I never learned my lessons
about rope-knots
and about getting home
in the absolute dark
by listening to what
the foot crumbles.
My next life may
be hopeless trying
like this one,
a sleepy clutch of
mosquito net.

Kid Tropic

Able to lie down wherever he
is put. The myth is movable.

A rose in his brain
has been wilting for centuries.

He is his
people's decline into the Pile
of Things.

        It's a boat in the end.

What you love steps onto
something moving away.

Able to learn a strange tongue
or two from Him that wrote.

Able to run into a forest with
good reason and only sandals on.

You might see him driving
with the top down or
talking to creatures in the dark

but he's at the end of
a fall down the stairs—

so far from home he's had to
take home with him.

Wherever he lives
an Ngorongoro.

Saith the Missionary

And so cross the river
as the Lord required
to glimpse of this Thing
obedient to Motions.

Remember to use your third eye
when going through
Fire and Water of mountain-gods.

This is what Samuel put strongly
in a lovely bit of forest
one might fairly reckon.

Poem by Leigh Hunt (1784-1859)

Some griefs are so gentle
in their nature. Of this
kind is the death of an infant
mistaken for a beautiful stone
posed by the nurse
in your exhausted arms.

You get flesh-quakes
sleeping next to your wife,
the thing between you dead.

I hope by my writing this
down just opposite a spot
on the page where a handprint is

a reasonable yielding
will come to us both.

Minus Time

I'm to be a credit to the Earth.
I had to let go of friends
who didn't want to get blown away
in a preposterous lozenge.

It's not so cold on the inside—
I've got my historical disadvantage,
the view of a grain of sand.

Stoop to enter the cabin.
Have some lemon peel to chew.
I'll take our hats, keep them safe
near these glass nothings.
You lean the walking sticks.
I guess it's a painting of Boudica.
Bring tea and biscuits.
I'm so full of the forest
and it's all hitting the spot.
My breaths are cavernous.

Notes

The book's epigraph is from Ghalib's Persian verse
and is found in *The Oxford India Ghalib*, edited
by Richard Russell. This treasury includes English
translations of Ghalib's Urdu and Persian verse as
well as the essay "Ghalib: Life and Letters" by Russell
and Kurshidul Islam. Reproduced with permission of
Oxford University Press India © Oxford University
Press. Unauthorized copying is strictly prohibited.

The two quotations of scripture are from J.A.
Rodwell's 1876 Second Revised and Amended Edition
El-Koran.

The epigraph for "Girl Without Limbs" concludes
the short story "My Mother, Her Crime" by Ambai,
translated by Lakshmi Holmström. The story is
available in *Her Story So Far: Tales of the Girl
Child in India*, edited by Monica Das and published
by Penguin India. Reproduced with permission of
Monica Das.

Poems in an identified voice were made by using
found and original work.

This book is for my wife and our parents.

About the Author

Ayaz Pirani was born in Musoma, Tanzania, to parents born in Kapsabet, Kenya, and Tanga, Tanzania. He grew up in Canada and studied Humanities and Writing at Collège Glendon in Toronto and Concordia University in Montreal. At Vermont College of Fine Arts, Pirani was a student of the late Jack Myers. *Happy You Are Here* is his first book. He lives near Monterey, California.

About The Word Works

The Word Works, a nonprofit literary organization, publishes contemporary poetry and presents public programs. Imprints include the Washington Prize, International Editions, and the Hilary Tham Capital Collection. A reading period is held in May.

Monthly, The Word Works offers free literary programs in the Chevy Chase, MD, Café Muse series, and each summer, it holds free poetry programs in Washington, D.C.'s Rock Creek Park. Annually in June, two high school students debut in the Joaquin Miller Poetry Series as winners of the Jacklyn Potter Young Poets Competition. Since 1974, Word Works programs have included: "In the Shadow of the Capitol," a symposium and archival project on the African American intellectual community in segregated Washington, D.C.; the Gunston Arts Center Poetry Series; the Poet Editor panel discussions at The Writer's Center; and Master Class workshops.

As a 501(c)3 organization, The Word Works has received awards from the National Endowment for the Arts, the National Endowment for the Humanities, the D.C. Commission on the Arts & Humanities, the Witter Bynner Foundation, Poets & Writers, The Writer's Center, Bell Atlantic, the David G. Taft Foundation, and others, including many generous private patrons.

The Word Works has established an archive of artistic and administrative materials in the Washington Writing Archive housed in the George Washington University Gelman Library. It is a member of the Community of Literary Magazines and Presses and its books are distributed by Small Press Distribution.

wordworksbooks.org

Other Word Works Books

Karren L. Alenier, *Wandering on the Outside*
Karren L. Alenier, ed., *Whose Woods These Are*
Karren L. Alenier & Miles David Moore, eds.,
  Winners: A Retrospective of the Washington Prize
Christopher Bursk, ed., *Cool Fire*
Grace Cavalieri, *Creature Comforts*
Barbara Goldberg, *Berta Broadfoot and Pepin the Short*
Frannie Lindsay, *If Mercy*
Marilyn McCabe, *Glass Factory*
W. T. Pfefferle, *My Coolest Shirt*
Jacklyn Potter, Dwaine Rieves, Gary Stein, eds.,
  Cabin Fever: Poets at Joaquin Miller's Cabin
Robert Sargent, *Aspects of a Southern Story*
  & *A Woman from Memphis*
Nancy White, ed., *Word for Word*

THE TENTH GATE PRIZE

Jennifer Barber, *Works on Paper*, 2015
Lisa Sewell, *Impossible Object*, 2014

THE HILARY THAM CAPITAL COLLECTION

Mel Belin, *Flesh That Was Chrysalis*
Carrie Bennett, *The Land Is a Painted Thing*
Doris Brody, *Judging the Distance*
Sarah Browning, *Whiskey in the Garden of Eden*
Grace Cavalieri, *Pinecrest Rest Haven*
Cheryl Clarke, *By My Precise Haircut*
Christopher Conlon, *Gilbert and Garbo in Love*
    & *Mary Falls: Requiem for Mrs. Surratt*
Donna Denizé, *Broken like Job*
W. Perry Epes, *Nothing Happened*
Bernadette Geyer, *The Scabbard of Her Throat*
Barbara G. S. Hagerty, *Twinzilla*
James Hopkins, *Eight Pale Women*
Brandon Johnson, *Love's Skin*
Marilyn McCabe, *Perpetual Motion*
Judith McCombs, *The Habit of Fire*
James McEwen, *Snake Country*
Miles David Moore, *The Bears of Paris*
    & *Rollercoaster*
Kathi Morrison-Taylor, *By the Nest*
Tera Vale Ragan, *Reading the Ground*
Michael Shaffner, *The Good Opinion of Squirrels*
Maria Terrone, *The Bodies We Were Loaned*
Hilary Tham, *Bad Names for Women*
    & *Counting*
Barbara Louise Ungar, *Charlotte Brontë, You Ruined My Life*
    & *Immortal Medusa*
Jonathan Vaile, *Blue Cowboy*
Rosemary Winslow, *Green Bodies*
Michele Wolf, *Immersion*
Joe Zealberg, *Covalence*

THE WASHINGTON PRIZE

Nathalie F. Anderson, *Following Fred Astaire*, 1998

Michael Atkinson, *One Hundred Children Waiting for a Train*, 2001

Molly Bashaw, *The Whole Field Still Moving Inside It*, 2013

Carrie Bennett, *biography of water*, 2004

Peter Blair, *Last Heat*, 1999

John Bradley, *Love-in-Idleness: The Poetry of Roberto Zingarello*, 1995,
    2ND edition 2014

Christopher Bursk, *The Way Water Rubs Stone*, 1988

Richard Carr, *Ace*, 2008

Jamison Crabtree, *Rel[AM]ent*, 2014

Barbara Duffey, *Simple Machines*, 2015

B. K. Fischer, *St. Rage's Vault*, 2012

Linda Lee Harper, *Toward Desire*, 1995

Ann Rae Jonas, *A Diamond Is Hard But Not Tough*, 1997

Frannie Lindsay, *Mayweed*, 2009

Richard Lyons, *Fleur Carnivore*, 2005

Elaine Magarrell, *Blameless Lives*, 1991

Fred Marchant, *Tipping Point*, 1993, 2ND edition 2013

Ron Mohring, *Survivable World*, 2003

Barbara Moore, *Farewell to the Body*, 1990

Brad Richard, *Motion Studies*, 2010

Jay Rogoff, *The Cutoff*, 1994

Prartho Sereno, *Call from Paris*, 2007, 2ND edition 2013

Enid Shomer, *Stalking the Florida Panther*, 1987

John Surowiecki, *The Hat City After Men Stopped Wearing Hats*, 2006

Miles Waggener, *Phoenix Suites*, 2002

Charlotte Warren, *Gandhi's Lap*, 2000

Mike White, *How to Make a Bird with Two Hands*, 2011

Nancy White, *Sun, Moon, Salt*, 1992, 2ND edition 2010

George Young, *Spinoza's Mouse*, 1996

INTERNATIONAL EDITIONS

Kajal Ahmad (Alana Marie Levinson-LaBrosse, Mewan
    Nahro Said Sofi, and Darya Abdul-Karim Ali Najin,
    trans., with Barbara Goldberg), *Handful of Salt*
Keyne Cheshire (trans.), *Murder at Jagged Rock: A Tragedy*
    by Sophocles
Yoko Danno & James C. Hopkins, *The Blue Door*
Moshe Dor, Barbara Goldberg, Giora Leshem, eds.,
    The Stones Remember: Native Israeli Poets
Moshe Dor (Barbara Goldberg, trans.), *Scorched by the Sun*
Lee Sang (Myong-Hee Kim, trans.), *Crow's Eye View:*
    The Infamy of Lee Sang, Korean Poet
Vladimir Levchev (Henry Taylor, trans.), *Black Book of*
    the Endangered Species